# UPPER CRUST

## BRENDA BELL

Contemporary Books, Inc.
Chicago • New York

*To Bill, Mama, and Douglas, who encouraged and believed.*

Copyright © 1986 by Brenda Bell
All rights reserved
Published by Contemporary Books, Inc.
180 North Michigan Avenue, Chicago, Illinois 60601
Manufactured in the United States of America
International Standard Book Number: 0-8092-4989-8

Published simultaneously in Canada by Beaverbooks, Ltd.
195 Allstate Parkway, Valleywood Business Park
Markham, Ontario L3R 4T8 Canada

# CONTENTS

INTRODUCTION  5

**1**
**BREAKFAST AND BRUNCH**  18

**2**
**MEATS**  30

**3**
**SEAFOOD AND POULTRY**  48

**4**
**GARDEN FAVORITES**  65

**5**
**MORE SENSATIONAL SANDWICHES**  76

INDEX  79

# INTRODUCTION

Sandwiches are sensational! They can be anything you want—hearty meat and cheese combinations, or fresh vegetables; open-face or closed; creamy, chewy, or crunchy; sweet or savory; hot or cold. The delicious possibilities are nearly endless.

Indeed, sandwiches have come a long way since the eighteenth century when legend has it that John Montagu, Fourth Earl of Sandwich, ordered two pieces of bread to "hold" some slices of roast meat so he could continue his card game without messing up the cards. No matter whether the Earl's fondness for gambling is really what we have to thank for the creation of the sandwich—it is a great culinary invention that has been a favorite ever since.

Known and loved for their simplicity and convenience, sandwiches also conjure images of "last minute," "impromptu," and "for kids." Even though some of the best sandwiches *are* impromptu—created from leftovers in the refrigerator and whatever else is on hand—sandwiches do not have to be an afterthought. A good sandwich meal deserves planning just as any other meal.

Sandwiches—at last—have shed that predictable, ordinary spur-of-the-moment image and emerged as great meals for family or guests, and for any meal occasion—lunch, brunch, supper, or snacks. They travel with the brown-bag crowd to the office and to school, they go on picnics, they appear on the menus of restaurants. Boring they're not—as you'll see from the recipes and sandwich combinations suggested here.

Recipes range from light snacks to hearty, nutritious meal-in-a-sandwich ideas. Most are very simple to prepare—many in less than half an hour. All are high on flavor and good eating appeal. Many use staple ingredients you are likely to have on hand; others feature ingredients easy to obtain on a quick trip to the supermarket. Still other ingredients—such as cooked chicken or turkey—may be left over from another meal. In fact, it's not a bad idea to plan to cook enough extras to provide sandwich makings.

A word to the nutrition-conscious. Sandwiches can score high as healthful meal choices. Whole-grain breads, fruits, and vegetables are a good source of complex carbohydrates, vitamins, and minerals. Poultry, fish, meat, cheeses, and many legumes are fine sources of protein. And smart accompaniment choices will round out a complete, nutritious meal.

## WHAT MAKES A GOOD SANDWICH

Breads, fillings, and spreads! It's that simple!

### Breads

A great sandwich begins with the right bread—one with the best flavor and texture to complement the sandwich filling and spread. Full-flavored ingredients such as roast beef and horseradish need a hearty, distinctive bread—thin-sliced, delicately textured bread just won't do. A more satisfying choice might be a hearty pumpernickel roll or a chewy-crusted French sourdough.

Fresh bread is the first step to a good sandwich. Most prepackaged breads will be coded with a sell date—which means the bread should be fresh for a couple of days beyond that date. Bakery breads, if not sold fresh on the day they are baked, should be marked as "day-old." (And your home-baked bread should be eaten fresh, too!) For those breads that you don't plan to use right away (or within a few days, according to the type of bread), freezing is probably the best way to store them to retain optimum freshness.

Of course, there really are no hard and fast rules for the breads you choose. Personal preference always needs to be considered. And don't give up on a recipe just because you don't have—or can't locate—the particular type of bread called for. Just substitute another type!

The variety of flavors, shapes, textures, and sizes of rolls and loaves available today is astounding. And with many people baking their own bread, there are many interesting homemade varieties. Unfortunately, all types of bread are not available everywhere—there are regional and ethnic specialties and preferences. Recipes in this book call for readily available breads, and alternatives are suggested for variety. But don't be limited by these choices—be flexible and adventurous! Consider other bread and roll suggestions:

- White
- Rye
- Pumpernickel
- Cinnamon
- Raisin
- French
- Italian
- Vienna

- Cuban
- Multigrain
- Bran
- Hard rolls
- Challah
- Oatmeal
- Potato
- Sourdough

- Cracked wheat
- Granola
- Whole wheat
- Kaiser rolls
- Egg
- Onion
- Cheese
- Herb

Or for a change of pace from the traditional bread slices or rolls, try one of these for a super sandwich:

- Bagels
- Croissants
- Muffins (Corn, Cranberry, Blueberry)
- Quick-bread slices (Date, Nut, Apple, Banana)
- Biscuits
- English muffins
- Brioches
- Pita breads
- Tortillas

**Fillings and Spreads**
Fillings (the meats, cheeses, salads, vegetables) are usually the major flavor components of the sandwich. Spreads add complementary flavors

to the fillings and breads, as well as keep the bread from becoming soggy. And sometimes the spread is used alone without any other filling.

Spreads—usually butter, mayonnaise, cream cheese, mustard—can be purchased or homemade. When seasoning ingredients are added to spreads, often they are made ahead to allow flavors to blend. If spreads (especially those with butter or cream cheese bases) have been refrigerated, make sure they are soft enough to spread evenly over the bread, otherwise the bread might tear.

Mustard has always been a favorite way to add a bit of zip and color to sandwiches. In case you haven't glanced around the mustard section of your grocery lately, these are some of the varieties you might find (in addition to the old standard yellow ballpark-type mustard). Choose mild or hot, sweet or spicy, smooth or grainy:

- Dijon
- Spicy
- Brown
- Pesto
- Herb
- Champagne
- Chili
- Creole
- Honey
- Chinese
- Düsseldorf
- Tarragon

. . . just to name a few!

It's easy to flavor mustards at home by adding favorite herbs (basil, tarragon, or chervil, for example) to a prepared mustard such as Dijon or a brown mustard. Or you can add chili powder, garlic powder, chutney, salsa, or honey—just choose a flavor to complement the sandwich and the mustard.

Mayonnaise is probably one of the most "reached for" spreads around. And the best, in many opinions, is homemade. The following is a fast, flavorful mayonnaise made in the food processor. Basic cookbooks abound with recipes for mayonnaise and flavor variations, so do a little experimenting to find the one that best suits your needs.

## BASIC MAYONNAISE

Makes about 1½ cups

- 1 large egg
- 2 tablespoons fresh lemon juice, white wine vinegar, or cider vinegar
- 1 teaspoon Dijon-style mustard (optional)
  White pepper, to taste
  Salt, to taste
- 1¼ cups olive or vegetable oil

Combine all ingredients except oil in food processor work bowl. Process to blend well, about 30 seconds. With motor running, slowly add oil in thin steady stream and process until thickened. Adjust seasonings. Store covered in refrigerator.

Many spreads and fillings in this book have a mayonnaise base to which other ingredients have been added. To make your own flavored mayonnaise, add minced onion, flavored vinegars, sour cream, yogurt, cheeses, herbs, and other seasonings. The idea is to subtly season the mayonnaise and still complement the other ingredients without overwhelming the basic filling flavor.

Cream cheese—plain, flavored, light, soft or whipped—makes a great spread. You can purchase flavored cream cheeses, but they are also simple to make, and so easy to make in the quantity you need. Most cream cheese spreads keep well, so it's a good idea to make double the amount you plan to use to have some on hand for other sandwiches. The mild, tangy flavor of cream cheese takes well to the addition of so many different flavors and textures—herbs, seasonings, spices, finely chopped vegetables, horseradish, chutney, nuts, dates, raisins, bacon, chopped pickles, grated lemon or orange zest, or honey.

Butter is another all-around favorite sandwich spread. For flavored butters, just stir your favorite seasoning into softened butter: minced garlic or onion, garlic or onion powder, celery salt, Parmesan cheese, paprika, seeds (poppy, toasted sesame, celery, or caraway), or any combination of herbs, dried or fresh, to complement the sandwich filling.

*Note:* Refrigerated butter or cream cheese is easily softened in the microwave oven if you're in a hurry and don't have time to soften it at room temperature.

- *Butter*—Place unwrapped butter in small bowl; microwave, uncovered, on LOW about 2 minutes.

- *Cream Cheese*—Place unwrapped cream cheese in small bowl; microwave uncovered, on LOW about 3 minutes.

**Sandwich Extras**

A few words about substitutions and ingredient changes. Go ahead! One of the great things about sandwiches is that there are no hard-and-fast rules. You can make changes in amounts and ingredients almost at will and the sandwich will still be a delicious success. Here are some suggestions:

- Add these "leaves" to sandwiches for extra crunch, color, flavor, and, in most cases, added nutritional value. Buy whatever is in season (or use whatever is in your garden) for best flavor and least expense. Some favorite sandwich leaves:

    Bibb lettuce
    Romaine lettuce
    Spinach
    Watercress
    Cabbage (green, red, savoy, or Chinese)
    Radicchio
    Leaf lettuce
    Iceberg lettuce
    Boston lettuce

- And other favorite extras:

    Tomatoes—any kind, including cherry tomatoes and yellow tomatoes

Onions—yellow, white, green, red
Pickles—dill, sweet, hot, mustard; in spears, slices, relish, or chopped; pickled vegetables
Sprouts—alfalfa, bean, radish
Zucchini—thinly slice lengthwise
Mushrooms—slice—leave raw or sauté; experiment with the exotic ones found in many markets
Peppers—sweet bell peppers (green, red, yellow, purple), hot peppers
Cheese—shred, cube, or slice as desired

## SANDWICH TIPS

**Hot and Cold Sandwiches**

Obviously, some sandwiches taste better cold, and some hot—but quite frequently they are good both ways. Experiment to determine your preferences.

Hot sandwiches may be grilled (in a skillet on the range top) or simply heated in the oven or microwave. Instructions are given in many recipes for oven heating, broiling, or stove-top grilling. If you prefer heating in the microwave, check your manufacturer's use manual for specific directions for your particular model.

Following are general guidelines for microwaving sandwiches:

Place sandwich in the microwave oven on a microwave-safe paper towel (the paper towel prevents bottom of sandwich from becoming soggy). Microwave on **HIGH** for about 15 seconds, just until sandwich is warm. Do not heat too long, or bread will become hard and other ingredients might also be adversely affected.

For a fun look and pleasing texture on grilled sandwiches, try a waffle iron. Butter the bread as you would for grilling, then place in waffle iron preheated according to manufacturer's directions. Heat sandwich 2 or 3 minutes or as manufacturer directs.

**For "Lighter" Dining**

Somewhere along the line, sandwiches acquired a bad reputation. Sandwiches don't have to be high-fat, high-sodium, calorie-laden meals. Just as with other foods, you can make sandwiches that fit your desire for a lighter repast.

For starters, use less meat and cheese. Use enough for flavor, but don't be too heavy-handed with these higher calorie, higher fat ingredients. Check out the numerous "lighter" products found in the supermarkets today. Look carefully, though, because "lighter" may mean reduced calories, lower fat, low-sodium, sodium-free, or something else—choose products that fit *your* needs. With "lighter" in mind, you might check out some of the following:

- Mayonnaise
- Salad dressings
- Margarines and spreads
- Cream cheese
- Sour cream substitutes
- Ham (often available with reduced fat and/or sodium)

And you can make other substitutions and changes such as:

- Use turkey, chicken, or turkey ham in place of beef or ham.
- Purchase low-fat or nonfat yogurt and use as mayonnaise extender or as a substitute for mayonnaise or sour cream.
- In recipes that call for vinaigrette-type dressings, try using less oil than is called for in a recipe, or substitute a commercial vinaigrette-type dressing that contains reduced oil or no oil. Add spices and seasonings suggested in recipe.
- Reduce or eliminate salt called for in a recipe.
- Grill sandwiches in a nonstick skillet without adding extra butter.
- Sauté in nonstick skillets and reduce the amount of fat called for in recipes.

**Take-Along Sandwiches**
Sandwiches make super portable fare for brown baggers and picnickers if you follow a few important guidelines:

- Most sandwiches are best if assembled just prior to eating, so whenever possible carry separately the bread, spreads, and crisp or juicy items such as tomatoes, pickles, and lettuce.
- Carry sandwiches that *can* be assembled ahead (either partially or completely) in plastic containers or well wrapped in plastic or foil.
- Many sandwich fillings and spreads—*especially* those containing ingredients such as mayonnaise, eggs, cream cheese, and poultry—

should be kept in a cold place such as an ice chest, cooler, or refrigerator until serving time.
- Pack hot fillings in vacuum bottles that have been warmed with hot water prior to adding the heated filling; assemble sandwich just before eating.

**More Tips For Great Sandwiches**
- Try toasting bread for a nice flavor and texture contrast.
- Immediately refrigerate any leftovers that are susceptible to spoilage if not to be used right away.
- Don't be limited when it comes to bread. Use more than one kind in the same sandwich for a great look and flavor variation. Team pumpernickel with white, or wheat with seeded rye bread.
- When cutting a sandwich in half will make it easier to eat, use a serrated knife and saw without pressing, to avoid tearing or crushing the bread.
- Spread mayonnaise, butter, and other spreads right to the edges of the bread to protect bread from a potentially soggy filling.
- Several thin slices of meat are easier to eat than one thick slice in a sandwich.
- Don't add too many moist ingredients before grilling a sandwich or you might end up with a soggy sandwich.
- When sandwich fillings call for cubes of meat or cheese, think about the type of bread being served to determine what size cubes will be most suitable.

- Be careful not to add too much filling to sandwiches—they could become impossibly messy to eat.

### AN IMPORTANT NOTE ON INGREDIENT AMOUNTS USED IN THIS BOOK

Conspicuously missing in some of the recipes in this book are amounts for sliced meats, poultry, and cheeses. Basically the amount used depends on personal preference, but there are general guidelines.

All sandwiches—unless otherwise specified in the recipe—were prepared with two to four ounces of thinly sliced meats or poultry per sandwich, or one or two ounces of cheese. When *both* cheese and meat or poultry are called for, you might want to use half and half—or one ounce of cheese to two to three ounces of meat.

In all recipes, consider the size of the bread you select before adding the amounts of spread and/or filling called for in the recipe. Remember that loaf and roll sizes vary, so your sandwich may require more or less than suggested in a recipe. If you are substituting a biscuit or bagel for rye bread, for example, you will probably need less filling and spread than was originally indicated in the recipe. To serve as a guideline for meal planning, most recipes suggest the number of sandwiches you can expect from the recipe, and, whenever possible, indicate the amount of filling and spread. Remember to consider appetite size, too—heartier appetites obviously require more of everything!

# 1
# BREAKFAST AND BRUNCH

These versatile sandwiches can star as early morning eye-openers or later morning brunch—and some make super snacks anytime. Eggs, fruit, cream cheese spreads, and other ingredients come together deliciously in these recipe ideas. Simple to prepare, they make stunning presentations you'll serve often.

MUSHROOM & LEEK CROISSANT
GINGER-APPLE TOPPER
ASPARAGUS GRATINEE
FRENCH TOAST A L'ORANGE
HONEY CREAM CHEESE CRUNCH
SUNRISE SALAD
CAMEMBERT AND PEAR CROISSANT
SUGAR & SPICE
BLUE CHEESE-WALNUT SPREAD
CHEVRE AND EGGS FLORENTINE
SMOKED SALMON AND WATERCRESS

# MUSHROOM & LEEK CROISSANT

*Scrambled eggs topped with mushrooms and leeks make a company-perfect breakfast.*

Makes 2 sandwiches

- 1 leek, cut into very thin 1-inch-long strips (about 1 cup)
- 1-2 tablespoons butter or margarine
- 1 cup thinly sliced fresh mushrooms
- 2 croissants
- 2 thin slices Canadian bacon, sautéed (optional)
- 4 eggs, soft-scrambled or as desired

Cook leek in butter in medium skillet over medium heat 2 minutes, stirring frequently. Add mushrooms. Continue cooking and stirring 1 minute or until mushrooms are tender. Split croissants horizontally. Place bacon slice on bottom half of each. Top each with eggs and mushroom-leek mixture. Top with remaining half of croissant.

*Bread Alternatives:* French or Vienna bread (cut into $\frac{3}{4}$-inch-thick slices). If desired, spread one side with softened butter or garlic butter, then toast under broiler; top with bacon, eggs, and mushroom-leek mixture. Serve open-face.

# GINGER-APPLE TOPPER

*Apples and spice are always nice for brunch. Serve with crisp bacon slices or honey-cured ham. The ginger cream cheese makes a delicious spread alone, too.*

Makes ⅓ cup cream cheese spread, or enough for 2–3 sandwiches

- 1 3-ounce package cream cheese, softened
- 1–2 tablespoons finely chopped crystallized ginger
- 2 tablespoons finely chopped toasted almonds
- 1–2 medium apples, sliced ¼ inch thick (use Granny Smith, Golden Delicious, or other favorite cooking apple)
- Butter or margarine (divided)
- 1–2 teaspoons brown sugar
- 2–3 slices Vienna bread, cut 1 inch thick
- Cinnamon sugar (optional)
- Vanilla yogurt (optional)

Combine cream cheese, ginger, and almonds; stir to mix well. Cook apples in 1–2 tablespoons butter in medium skillet over medium heat until as tender as desired; stir occasionally. Sprinkle with brown sugar; continue cooking and stirring to dissolve sugar. Spread one side of each bread slice lightly with softened butter; sprinkle with cinnamon sugar if desired. Broil just until bread is lightly toasted. Spread each slice with ginger–cream cheese mixture. Arrange apples over cream cheese. Serve immediately, topped with yogurt.

*Bread Alternatives:* croissants, English muffins, or whole wheat bread (cut into 1-inch-thick slices).

# ASPARAGUS GRATINEE

*Stack it any way you like—it's a delicious combination, colorful and flavor-filled.*

Makes 2 sandwiches

- 2 thin slices ham or Canadian bacon, sautéed
- 2 thin tomato slices
- 1 hard-cooked egg, sliced
- 2-4 asparagus spears, cooked crisp-tender
- 1 English muffin, split and toasted
- 2 slices Gruyère, white cheddar, or Monterey Jack cheese

Layer ham, tomato, egg, and asparagus (trimmed to fit if necessary) on each muffin half. Top each with cheese slice. Broil just until cheese begins to melt.

If you wish, creamy blue cheese salad dressing can be substituted for cheese slice. Spoon desired amount over sandwich and broil briefly to heat.

*Bread Alternatives:* whole wheat bread (cut into ¾-inch-thick slices) or Vienna bread (cut into ¾-inch-thick slices).

# FRENCH TOAST A L'ORANGE

*Breakfast never tasted so good!*

Makes 2 sandwiches

- 4 slices raisin bread
- ¼ cup Orange Cream Cheese (to prepare, see Cranberry Turkey Croissant)
- 2 eggs
- 2 tablespoons milk
- 1 tablespoon orange-flavored liqueur (optional)
- 2-3 tablespoons butter or margarine
- Confectioners sugar
- **Orange marmalade, raspberry or strawberry preserves, or maple syrup**

Spread two slices raisin bread with cream cheese (about 2 tablespoons each). Top with remaining two slices bread; press together. Beat together eggs, milk, and liqueur. Dip each sandwich into egg mixture, turning to coat both sides. Cook in butter in large skillet over medium heat until lightly browned; turn and repeat. Sprinkle with sugar. Serve with marmalade, preserves, or syrup.

*Bread Alternative:* Vienna bread slices (cut about ¾ inch thick).

# HONEY CREAM CHEESE CRUNCH

*Great for breakfast or snacks! Tuck thin slices of apple into sandwich for extra crunch.*

Makes ½ cup cream cheese spread

- 1 4-ounce container whipped cream cheese
- 2-3 teaspoons honey
- 3 tablespoons raisins, chopped if desired
- 3 tablespoons toasted chopped walnuts or pecans
- ¼ teaspoon ground cinnamon (optional)
- **Bagels, split and toasted**

Combine all ingredients except bagels; stir to mix well. Spread about 2 tablespoons cream cheese mixture onto bottom half of bagel; top with remaining half. Store extra spread in refrigerator for later use.

*Bread Alternatives:* toasted pitas (cut in half to form pockets; spread 2 tablespoons filling in each pocket), toasted whole wheat English muffins, quick bread slices (nut, orange, cranberry, banana, apple), muffins (corn, blueberry, banana, plain).

# SUNRISE SALAD

*A zesty egg salad, with lots of flavor variations to suit everyone's taste. Makes a great breakfast!*

Makes 2 cups salad, or enough for 2-3 sandwiches

- 4 hard-cooked eggs, chopped
- ¼ cup finely chopped celery
- 2 green onions, finely chopped
- 2 tablespoons finely chopped red or green bell pepper
- ⅓ cup mayonnaise
- 3 tablespoons sour cream or plain yogurt
- 1-2 tablespoons prepared horseradish
- 1½ teaspoons celery seeds
- Salt and pepper, as desired
- Dash cayenne
- 4-6 slices pumpernickel bread, cut ¾ inch thick, toasted if desired

Gently stir together eggs, celery, onions, and pepper. Combine mayonnaise, sour cream, horseradish, celery seeds, salt, pepper, and cayenne; stir to mix well. Add to egg mixture and stir gently to combine. Spread filling on two or three slices of bread; top each with second bread slice.

*Variations:* Bacon—top egg salad with sautéed slices of Canadian bacon or crisp bacon strips. Dill—omit horseradish and celery seeds. Add 1 teaspoon dried dill weed. Olive—omit celery seeds. Add ⅓ cup sliced pitted ripe olives. Pickle—add 2–3 tablespoons finely chopped sweet or dill pickles. Almond—add 2–3 tablespoons toasted slivered almonds.

*Bread Alternatives:* white bread, bagels, English muffins, whole wheat bread, or pita breads.

## CAMEMBERT AND PEAR CROISSANT
*Simple but special! Elegant for brunch with a glass of white wine.*
Makes 2 sandwiches

> **2 croissants**
> **Camembert cheese**
> **Smoked turkey slices**
> **Bosc pear (cut into very thin slices)**

Split croissants horizontally. Cut ¼-inch slices of Camembert and place on bottom half of croissant. Broil just to melt cheese slightly. (Toast inside top halves of croissants also if desired.) Layer turkey and pear over cheese. Top with remaining half of croissant.

*Variation:* Substitute other favorite pear if desired.

# SUGAR & SPICE

*A quick "cheese toast" that's a bit unusual, but so good!*

Makes 1 cup cottage cheese spread, or enough for 2–4 sandwiches

- 1 cup cream-style cottage cheese
- ½ teaspoon ground cinnamon
- 2 tablespoons raisins or chopped walnuts
- 1 tablespoon brown sugar
- 2–4 slices whole wheat bread, cut ½ inch thick
- Brown sugar

Combine cottage cheese and cinnamon. Stir in raisins or nuts and 1 tablespoon brown sugar. Divide cheese mixture evenly among bread slices, spreading to ½ inch from edges of bread. (Use 3–4 slices if bread is small; cottage cheese mixture should not be too thick, or it will not heat completely during broiling.) Sprinkle lightly and evenly with additional brown sugar. Broil about 6 inches from heat source, until sugar melts and edges of bread are toasted. Check often for doneness, as sugar burns easily. Serve immediately.

*Bread Alternatives:* oatmeal bread, granola bread, or white bread.

# BLUE CHEESE-WALNUT SPREAD

*This delicious combination of flavors and textures makes a stunning presentation, pleasing to the eye as well as the palate.*

Makes about ⅓ cup blue cheese spread, or enough for 3–4 sandwiches

- **1 3-ounce package cream cheese, softened**
- **1–2 ounces blue cheese, crumbled**
- **2 tablespoons chopped toasted walnuts**
- **3–4 English muffins, split and toasted**
- **2 slices bacon, cooked crisp and crumbled**
- **Thin slices of pear or apple**

Combine cream cheese, blue cheese, and walnuts; stir to mix well. Spread blue cheese mixture on bottom half of each muffin. Top with bacon and pear slices, then with remaining half of muffin.

*Bread Alternatives:* toasted bagels, French or Italian bread loaf (cut into 3-inch lengths, then split horizontally), or pita breads.

# CHEVRE AND EGGS FLORENTINE

*Goat cheeses—made from goat's milk—are called chevres. They boast a zippy flavor that's a delicious breakfast choice to team with scrambled eggs.*

Makes 2 sandwiches

- 2 cups coarsely torn spinach leaves, tightly packed
- 2 tablespoons butter or margarine
- 4 eggs, beaten
- ¼ cup crumbled goat cheese
- 2 slices Vienna bread, cut ¾ inch thick, toasted
- 2 tablespoons finely chopped tomato

Cook spinach in 1 tablespoon butter in medium skillet over medium-low heat just until wilted; remove from skillet. Add remaining 1 tablespoon butter (or more if needed) to skillet. Add eggs. Cook over medium-low heat until eggs begin to set on bottom and sides; lift and fold to allow uncooked portion to set. Continue cooking until eggs are soft-scrambled; stir in cheese. Layer each toast slice with half of spinach, egg and cheese mixture, and tomato. Serve open-face.

*Bread Alternatives:* onion bread (cut into ¾-inch-thick slices), rye bread (cut into ¾-inch-thick slices), or wheat bread (cut into ¾-inch-thick slices).

# SMOKED SALMON AND WATERCRESS

*Cream cheese and smoked salmon pair up for an easy and delicious spread to serve for breakfast or brunch.*

Makes about ⅓ cup spread, or enough for 3–4 sandwiches

- 1 3-ounce package cream cheese, softened
- Dash lemon juice
- Dash hot pepper sauce
- 1–2 ounces smoked salmon
- Milk
- 1 green onion, minced (optional)
- 3–4 bagels, split, toasted if desired
- Watercress

Combine cream cheese, lemon juice, hot pepper sauce, and salmon in work bowl of food processor. Process until mixture is smooth. Add milk if mixture is too thick. Stir in onion by hand. Spread salmon mixture on bottom half of each bagel and top with watercress. Top with remaining half of bagel, or serve open-face, if preferred.

*Bread Alternatives:* English muffins, rye rolls, or French bread loaf (cut into 2- or 3-inch lengths, then split horizontally and serve open-face).

# 2
# MEATS

A main-dish sandwich to please most any palate—from hearty roast beef and blue cheese to an unusual twist to ham and Swiss—can be found here. There are sure to be several variations to your liking. Use these recipes as a starting point for spurring your sandwich imagination and create your own great combinations.

**PUMPERNICKEL GRILL**
**HONEY HAM SALAD**
**THE CHALET**
**GRILLED CARAWAY & HAM**
**THE ULTIMATE**
**OPEN-FACE STEAK & MUSHROOMS**
**TANGY BEEF STRIPS**
**PICADILLO PITA**
**REGAL ROQUEFORT**
**TACO PITA**
**NEVER-BETTER CORNED BEEF**
**DELI DELIGHT**
**ANTIPASTO PASSION**
**POLISH SAUSAGE 'N' KRAUT**
**SUPPER SAUSAGE SUPREME**
**CHUTNEY LAMB**

# PUMPERNICKEL GRILL

*The filling ingredients might sound a bit unusual, but try it for a unique taste treat.*

Makes ⅓ cup filling, or enough for 2 sandwiches

- 3 tablespoons mayonnaise
- 2 tablespoons canned chopped green chilies, well drained
- 2 slices bacon, cooked crisp and crumbled
- 1 green onion, finely chopped (green part only)
- Spicy mustard (optional)
- 4 slices pumpernickel bread, cut ½ inch thick
- 4 slices Monterey Jack cheese
- Butter or margarine, softened

Stir together mayonnaise, chilies, bacon, and onion. Spread mustard on two bread slices. Top each with one cheese slice, half the chili filling and a second cheese slice; then top with second slice of bread. Spread outsides of bread lightly with softened butter. Place sandwiches in large skillet over medium heat. Cook 3 minutes or until toasted; turn and cook 3 minutes longer until bread is toasted and filling is warm. Reduce heat if necessary to prevent overbrowning.

*Variation:* Spread mustard on one side of bread. Top with cheese slice, half of chili filling, and a tomato slice. Broil about 5 inches from heat source, just until heated through and cheese begins to melt. Serve open-face.

*Bread Alternatives:* whole wheat (cut into ½-inch-thick slices) or white (cut into ½-inch-thick slices).

# HONEY HAM SALAD

*A hearty salad—great made from leftover ham. In season, juicy ripe tomato slices are a nice addition.*

Makes 2 cups salad, or enough for 2 sandwiches

  ½ cup mayonnaise
  1 tablespoon lemon juice
  1 tablespoon prepared mustard (spicy brown or other favorite flavor)
  2 teaspoons honey
  ¼ cup finely chopped sweet pickles, drained well
1¾ cups cooked ham, cut into thin strips
  ¼ cup finely chopped celery
  2 tablespoons minced green onion
  2 pita breads, about 6 inches in diameter
    Lettuce or spinach leaves
    Ripe tomato slices (optional)

Combine mayonnaise, lemon juice, mustard, and honey. Stir in pickles. Combine ham, celery, and onion. Gently toss with mayonnaise mixture. Heat or toast pitas if desired. Cut each in half to form pockets. Line pockets with lettuce and tomato slices. Fill with ham salad.

*Bread Alternatives:* whole wheat sandwich rolls or onion rolls.

## CURRIED CHICKEN SALAD
*Chicken, celery, apple, and toasted almonds*

## OPEN-FACE STEAK AND MUSHROOMS
*Sirloin, mushrooms, and garlic toast*

## CAMEMBERT AND PEAR CROISSANT
*Camembert, pear, and turkey*

**FRENCH TOAST A L'ORANGE**
*Cream cheese, orange marmalade, and raisin bread*

# THE CHALET

*Ham and Swiss, tossed with spinach and a light vinaigrette, is a great make-ahead filling. For variety, try your favorite bottled sweet 'n' sour salad dressing instead.*

Makes about 3 cups ham mixture, or enough for 3-4 sandwiches

- 1 cup cooked ham, cut into 1-inch × ¼-inch strips
- 4 ounces Swiss cheese, cubed
- 1 small red onion, thinly sliced and separated into rings
- 2 tablespoons chopped parsley
- 3 tablespoons red wine vinegar
- 1½ teaspoons sugar
- Salt and pepper to taste
- ¼ cup vegetable oil
- 1 cup shredded spinach leaves
- 3-4 hard rolls
- Tomato slices (optional)

Combine ham, cheese, onion, and parsley. Stir together vinegar, sugar, salt, and pepper; whisk in oil. Add to ham mixture; toss to coat thoroughly. (If desired, refrigerate at this point several hours to allow flavors to blend, stirring occasionally.) Stir in shredded spinach just before serving. Split rolls horizontally; hollow out bottom portion slightly. Fill with ham mixture and add tomato slices. Top with remaining half of roll.

*Bread Alternatives:* rye bread or rolls or whole wheat bread or rolls.

# GRILLED CARAWAY & HAM

*Another twist to ham and Swiss!*

Makes ⅓ cup cream cheese spread, or enough for 3–4 sandwiches

   1   **3-ounce package cream cheese, softened**
3–4   **tablespoons country-style Dijon-style mustard (or other favorite)**
1½   **teaspoons caraway seeds, or to taste**
6–8   **slices rye bread, cut ½ inch thick**
3–4   **slices Swiss cheese**
       **Ham slices**
       **Red onion rings, very thinly sliced**
       **Butter or margarine, softened**

Combine cream cheese, mustard, and caraway seeds; stir to mix well. Spread cream cheese mixture on one side of all bread slices. With cream cheese side up, layer Swiss cheese, ham, and onion rings on half of the bread slices. Top with remaining bread, cream cheese side down. Spread outsides of bread lightly with butter. Place in large skillet over medium heat. Cook about 3 minutes until toasted; turn and cook 3 minutes longer, or until bread is toasted and filling is warm. Reduce heat if necessary to prevent overbrowning.

   *Note:* This sandwich may also be served cold, without grilling. Toast bread, if desired.

*Variations:* Butter Spread—Omit cream cheese; use ¼ cup softened butter or margarine and proceed as above. Sautéed Onion—Substitute 1 to 2 tablespoons sautéed onions for the red onion rings; proceed as above.

*Bread Alternatives:* pumpernickel or toasted English muffins.

# THE ULTIMATE

*So easy—but wait until you taste the blending of flavors!*

Makes about ¼ cup sandwich spread, or enough for 2 sandwiches

- 2 tablespoons mayonnaise
- 1 tablespoon chili sauce, catsup, or salsa
- 1 tablespoon finely chopped green or red bell pepper
- 1 tablespoon chopped chives
- 4 slices Muenster cheese
- Roast beef slices
- Crumbled cooked bacon
- 4 slices rye bread, cut ½ inch thick

Combine mayonnaise, chili sauce, pepper, and chives. Stir to mix well. Layer half of cheese, beef, mayonnaise mixture, and bacon on bread slice. Top with second slice of bread. Repeat for second sandwich. Wrap in foil. Place in 350°F oven for 15 minutes or until heated through.

*Variation:* Assemble sandwich as above. Spread outsides of bread lightly with softened butter or margarine. Place sandwiches in large skillet over medium heat. Cook 3 minutes or until toasted; turn and cook 3 minutes longer, or until bread is toasted and filling is warm. Reduce heat if necessary to prevent overbrowning.

*Bread Alternatives:* white, (cut into ½-inch-thick slices), onion rolls, or sourdough rolls.

# OPEN-FACE STEAK & MUSHROOMS

*For beef lovers everywhere. A great company meal idea, too—serve with a salad and glass of red wine.*

Makes 2 sandwiches

- 1 tablespoon softened butter
- Garlic powder, to taste
- Minced parsley, to taste
- 2 slices Vienna or French bread, cut 1 inch thick
- 1/2 pound boneless beef sirloin, cut into thin strips
- 1-2 tablespoons vegetable oil
- 1 1/2 cups sliced mushrooms
- Chopped green onion or chives

Combine butter, garlic powder, and parsley. Spread on one side of each bread slice; reserve. Cook beef in oil in medium skillet over medium heat about 2 minutes, stirring constantly. Add mushrooms and a dash of garlic powder. Continue cooking and stirring about 1 minute or until beef and mushrooms reach desired doneness. While beef is cooking, broil buttered bread slices just until toasted. Spoon beef-mushroom mixture evenly over the two slices. Sprinkle with green onion. Serve immediately.

*Bread Alternatives:* pumpernickel (cut into 1-inch-thick slices), rye (cut into 1-inch-thick slices), or wheat (cut into 1-inch-thick slices).

# TANGY BEEF STRIPS

*Horseradish and beef, the perennial favorites, star as a great sandwich duo.*

Makes 1 cup filling, or enough for 2 sandwiches

- 2 tablespoons red wine vinegar
- 1 tablespoon prepared horseradish, or to taste
- 1 tablespoon minced green onion
- ½ teaspoon sugar
- ½ teaspoon dry mustard
- Freshly ground black pepper
- 3 tablespoons vegetable oil
- 1 cup rare roast beef strips (about 6-8 ounces)
- 1 medium tomato, chopped (optional)
- 2 onion rolls
- Leaf lettuce

Stir together vinegar, horseradish, onion, sugar, mustard, and pepper. Whisk in oil. Add beef strips, and toss to coat thoroughly. Add tomato; toss gently. Split rolls horizontally. Layer lettuce and beef filling on bottom half of each roll. Top with remaining half of roll.

*Bread Alternatives:* pita breads, onion bagels, or hard rolls.

# PICADILLO PITA

*It's hard to say whether you will prefer the pita or corn bread variation for this slightly sweet filling. Try them both—each is a real flavor treat.*

Makes about 4 cups filling, or enough for 4 sandwiches

- 1 pound lean ground beef
- 1 medium onion, chopped
- 1 garlic clove, minced
- 1 16-ounce can stewed tomatoes
- 1 tablespoon vinegar
- ½ teaspoon ground cinnamon
- ½ teaspoon chili powder
- Dash ginger
- Salt (optional)
- ½ cup raisins
- 1 4-ounce can chopped green chilies, drained
- ¼ cup chopped pitted ripe olives
- ¼ cup toasted slivered almonds
- 4 pita breads, about 6 inches in diameter

Cook beef, onion, and garlic in medium skillet over medium heat until beef is no longer pink. Drain off any excess fat. Stir in tomatoes, vinegar, cinnamon, chili powder, ginger, salt, raisins, and chilies. Simmer, uncovered, until thickened, about 20 minutes. Stir in olives and almonds. Cut each pita in half to form pockets. Fill with picadillo mixture.

*Bread Alternatives:* corn bread squares or slices (spoon picadillo over; serve open-face), or tortillas.

# REGAL ROQUEFORT

*Delicious in a hot sandwich!*

Makes ¼ cup spread, or enough for 2 sandwiches

- ¼ **cup crumbled Roquefort**
- 2 **tablespoons butter or margarine, softened**
- **Dash garlic powder**
- 2 **onion rolls**
- **Roast beef slices**
- ¼ **cup sautéed onions, or to taste (optional)**

Combine cheese, butter, and garlic powder; stir to mix well. Split onion rolls horizontally. Spread cheese mixture on bottom half of roll; layer with roast beef and onions. Top with remaining half of roll and wrap in foil. Place in 350°F oven for 15 minutes or until heated through.

*Variation:* Substitute ham for the roast beef.

*Bread Alternatives:* sourdough rolls, bagels, or hard rolls.

# TACO PITA

*Serve tacos in pita pockets for a fun variation on an old favorite.*

Makes 2 cups filling, or enough for 2 sandwiches

- 1 pound ground beef
- 1 medium onion, chopped
- 2 garlic cloves, minced
- 2 teaspoons chili powder
- 1 teaspoon ground cumin
- Salt (optional)
- 1 8-ounce can tomato sauce
- 1 4-ounce can chopped green chilies, drained (optional)
- 2 pita breads, about 6 inches in diameter
- Chunky Guacamole (see page 73)
- Chopped tomatoes
- Shredded lettuce
- Sour cream
- Shredded cheddar cheese

Cook beef, onion, and garlic in medium skillet over medium heat until beef is no longer pink. Drain off any excess fat. Stir in chili powder, cumin, and salt to taste. Stir in tomato sauce and chilies. Simmer until thickened (about 20 minutes), stirring occasionally. Cut each pita in half to form pockets. Fill with taco mixture. Top as desired with Chunky Guacamole, tomatoes, lettuce, sour cream, and cheese.

*Bread Alternatives:* flour tortillas, taco shells, or corn bread squares (serve open-face).

# NEVER-BETTER CORNED BEEF

*A creamy, cheesy, tangy spread gives a new dimension to corned beef.*

Makes ½ cup spread or enough for 2–3 sandwiches

- 1 3-ounce package cream cheese, softened
- ¼ cup shredded Swiss cheese
- 1–2 tablespoons prepared horseradish
- 2 tablespoons minced parsley (optional)
- Butter or margarine, softened
- 4–6 slices rye bread, cut ¾ inch thick
- Thinly sliced corned beef
- Sauerkraut, rinsed and drained well (optional)

Combine cream cheese, Swiss cheese, horseradish, and parsley; stir to mix well. Spread 1–2 tablespoons cheese mixture on one side of each bread slice. With cheese side up, layer corned beef and sauerkraut on half of bread slices. Top with remaining bread, cheese side down. Spread outsides of bread lightly with butter. Place in large skillet over medium heat. Cook about 3 minutes, or until toasted; turn and cook 3 minutes longer, or until bread is toasted and filling is warm. Reduce heat if necessary to prevent overbrowning.

*Note:* This sandwich may also be served cold, without grilling. Toast bread if desired.

*Bread Alternatives:* pumpernickel, onion rolls, rye bagels, or toasted English muffins.

# DELI DELIGHT

*You'll want to keep plenty of this versatile cream cheese spread on hand. It's great as a spread on bagels and English muffins.*

Makes ⅓ cup cream cheese spread, or enough for 3–4 sandwiches

- **1 3-ounce package cream cheese, softened**
- **1 tablespoon chopped onion**
- **1 tablespoon finely chopped celery**
- **1 tablespoon finely chopped green pepper**
- **1 teaspoon prepared mustard**
- **6-8 slices whole wheat bread, cut ¾ inch thick**
  - **Ham, corned beef, turkey, or pastrami slices (or your preferred cold cuts)**
- **6-8 slices Swiss cheese (or other favorite)**
  - **Tomato slices**
  - **Spinach leaves or lettuce**

Combine cream cheese, onion, celery, green pepper, and mustard; stir to mix well. Spread desired amount on one side of each bread slice. Layer cold cut choices, Swiss cheese, tomato, and spinach on half of bread slices, cream cheese side up. Top with remaining bread, cream cheese side down.

*Bread Alternatives:* onion rolls, French bread or rolls, rye bread, bagels, or English muffins.

# ANTIPASTO PASSION

*Enjoy your favorite antipasto flavors in a roll! The filling can be prepared ahead and refrigerated—but let it stand a few minutes to take the chill off before making sandwiches. Sprinkle with Parmesan cheese, if you like.*

Makes 3 cups filling, or enough for 3–4 sandwiches

- ¼ pound salami, cut into 1-inch × ¼-inch strips
- 1 6-ounce jar marinated artichoke hearts, drained and coarsely chopped
- 1 medium red or green bell pepper, cut into thin strips
- ¼ pound mozzarella or provolone cheese, cut into ½-inch cubes
- Italian-style salad dressing
- 3–4 hard rolls
- **Romaine lettuce leaves**
- **Parmesan cheese (optional)**

Combine salami, artichokes, pepper strips, and cheese. Toss with dressing to moisten. Serve immediately or chill several hours for later use. To serve, split rolls horizontally and hollow out bottom portion slightly. Line bottom half of roll with lettuce. Fill with salami mixture. Sprinkle with Parmesan, if desired.

*Bread Alternatives:* pita breads or French or Italian bread loaf (cut into 4-inch lengths, then split horizontally).

# POLISH SAUSAGE 'N' KRAUT

*A robust sandwich; serve with fruit and a frosty mug of beer.*

Makes 3 cups filling, or enough for 3–4 sandwiches

- **1** garlic clove, minced
- **2** medium onions, sliced
- **2** tablespoons vegetable oil
- **2** cups sauerkraut, rinsed and drained
- **½** cup beer
- **1** teaspoon paprika
- **¾** pound precooked Polish kielbasa or other smoked sausage, cut into ¼-inch pieces
- French or Italian bread loaf
- Hearty mustard (optional)
- Caraway seeds (optional)
- Sour cream (optional)

Cook garlic and onions in oil in medium skillet over medium heat until tender and slightly browned. Add sauerkraut and beer. Increase heat; cook to reduce liquid. Stir in paprika and sausage. Simmer, uncovered, to heat sausage, about 5 minutes. Cut bread into 4-inch lengths; split each horizontally. Spread bottom half of each slice with mustard; top with sausage mixture. Sprinkle with caraway seeds and add a dollop of sour cream, if desired. Top with remaining half of bread.

*Bread Alternatives:* hard rolls, onion rolls, rye rolls, hearty rye or pumpernickel (cut into 1-inch-thick slices).

# SUPPER SAUSAGE SUPREME

*Italian sausage is an ever-popular sandwich fixing. A sprinkling of Parmesan and a dash of red pepper flakes add even more zip to this tasty version.*

Makes 3 cups filling, or enough for 3–4 sandwiches

- 3/4 pound mild or hot Italian sausage
- 1–2 tablespoons olive oil
- 2 medium onions, sliced
- 1 garlic clove, minced
- 1 cup green or red bell pepper strips (optional)
- **Italian or French bread loaf**
- **Parmesan cheese (optional)**
- **Red pepper flakes (optional)**

Cook sausage in medium skillet over medium heat until well browned. Remove sausage from skillet and pour off fat. Cut sausage into 1-inch pieces; reserve. Add oil to skillet, then add onions and garlic. Return sausage to skillet. Cook uncovered over medium heat, stirring occasionally, about 5 minutes. Cover and continue cooking, stirring occasionally, until sausages are cooked through, about 20 minutes. Stir in bell pepper strips during the last 5 or 10 minutes of cooking. Cut bread into 4-inch lengths. Split each horizontally; hollow out bottom portion slightly. Fill with sausage mixture. Sprinkle with Parmesan cheese and red pepper flakes, if desired. Top with remaining half of bread.

*Bread Alternatives:* pita breads, onion rolls, hard rolls, or sourdough rolls.

# CHUTNEY LAMB

*Chutney and ground lamb make an elegant entrée.*

Makes 2 servings

- ½ pound ground lamb
- 2 tablespoons minced green onion
- ½ teaspoon ground cumin
- ½ teaspoon ground coriander
- ⅛ teaspoon ground ginger
- ½ cup coarsely chopped red bell pepper
- 1 tablespoon butter or margarine
- ⅓ cup chutney, chopped if pieces are large
- 2 sandwich rolls, split, toasted if desired
- Lettuce leaves
- Salt
- Freshly ground black pepper

Gently stir together lamb, onion, cumin, coriander, and ginger. Shape into two patties about ½ to ¾ inch thick. Broil about 6 inches from heat source or panfry on medium-low heat about 5 minutes; turn and continue cooking until patties are of desired doneness. Meanwhile, cook bell pepper in butter in small skillet over medium-low heat until crisp-tender; drain excess fat. Stir in chutney; heat through. Line bottom half of each roll with lettuce. Place lamb patty on lettuce. Season with salt and pepper. Spread with chutney mixture and top with remaining half of roll, or serve open-face if desired.

*Bread Alternatives:* whole wheat rolls, onion rolls, toasted English muffin halves, or toasted French bread slices (serve open-face).

# 3
# SEAFOOD AND POULTRY

These sandwiches go beyond the traditional tuna and chicken salad. They are loaded with exciting flavor combinations destined to become favorites. A light ginger-laced Oriental chicken salad, or tuna with Italian flair, are just the beginning. Try them, then experiment to make your own new poultry and seafood creations.

**THE GREAT SALMON CAPER**
**CALIFORNIA DREAMIN'**
**PITA PROVENÇAL**
**TUNA CAPONATA**
**TURKEY & CHEDDAR PITA**
**TURKEY WITH HONEY-MUSTARD**
**CRANBERRY-TURKEY CROISSANT**
**PESTO CHICKEN**
**SUNFLOWER CHICKEN SALAD**
**TANGY DILL CHICKEN SALAD**
**TARRAGON CHICKEN CROISSANT**
**CURRIED CHICKEN SALAD**
**THE GREAT GARBANZO**
**GINGER CHICKEN PITA**

## THE GREAT SALMON CAPER
*Salmon, green onions, yogurt, capers, and chopped dill*

## CALIFORNIA DREAMIN'
*Shrimp, avocado, bacon, and celery*

# GINGER CHICKEN PITA
*Chicken, bean sprouts, celery, carrots, and green onion*

# THE GREAT SALMON CAPER

*Use leftover or canned salmon for this refreshing and attractive sandwich.*

Makes 2 cups salmon mixture, or enough for 4 sandwiches

- 1/4 cup plain yogurt (mayonnaise may be substituted)
- 2 tablespoons mayonnaise
- 1 tablespoon lemon juice
- Dash cayenne pepper
- Salt (optional)
- 1 15 1/2-ounce can pink or red salmon, drained and flaked, bones removed; or 2 cups cooked salmon, flaked and bones removed
- 1-2 green onions, finely chopped
- 1-2 tablespoons capers, well drained
- 2-3 teaspoons finely chopped fresh dill *or* 1 teaspoon dried dill weed
- 8 slices Vienna bread, cut 1/2 inch thick

Combine yogurt, mayonnaise, lemon juice, cayenne, and salt; stir to mix well. Gently stir in salmon, onions, capers, and dill. Divide filling among four slices of bread; top each with second bread slice.

*Bread Alternatives:* pita breads, hard rolls (hollow out bottom portion slightly), whole wheat rolls or bread, onion rolls, or toasted English muffins (serve open-face).

# CALIFORNIA DREAMIN'

*Finely chopped sweet pickles are a tasty addition to the filling.*

Makes about 2½ cups shrimp filling, or enough for 3-4 sandwiches

- ⅓ cup mayonnaise
- 2 tablespoons lemon juice
- 2 tablespoons minced parsley
- 1 tablespoon Dijon-style mustard
- Dash red pepper flakes
- ½ pound cooked shrimp, shelled and deveined, chilled
- ½ cup thinly sliced celery
- 4 strips bacon, cooked crisp and crumbled (optional)
- 2 green onions, minced
- 1 small avocado, cubed
- Freshly ground black pepper
- 3-4 sourdough rolls
- Spinach leaves

Combine mayonnaise, lemon juice, parsley, mustard, and red pepper flakes; stir to mix well. Combine shrimp, celery, bacon, onions, and avocado. Add mayonnaise mixture and toss to coat thoroughly. Add black pepper to taste. Split rolls horizontally; hollow out bottom portion slightly. Line bottom half of roll with spinach leaves. Fill with shrimp mixture. Top with remaining half of roll.

*Note:* If shrimp filling is made ahead, add bacon and avocado just before serving to prevent soggy bacon and darkening of avocado.

*Bread Alternatives:* French or Italian bread loaf (cut into 4-inch lengths, then split horizontally), onion rolls, whole wheat rolls, or pita breads.

# PITA PROVENÇAL

*A quick pizza-style meal—the anchovy lover's delight!*

Makes 2 servings

- 2 medium onions, thinly sliced
- 1 garlic clove, minced
- 2 tablespoons olive oil
- 2 pita breads, about 6 inches in diameter
- 4 anchovy fillets, or to taste
- ½ teaspoon dried oregano, crumbled
- 2 tablespoons finely chopped pitted ripe olives
- ¼ cup shredded Swiss cheese, or to taste
- 2 tablespoons grated Parmesan cheese

Cook onions and garlic in oil in medium skillet over medium-low heat until onions are tender and lightly browned, about 15 minutes. Reduce heat if necessary to prevent overbrowning. Divide onion mixture evenly between two pita rounds, spreading almost to the edges of each round. (Do *not* cut pocket; these are open-face sandwiches.) Arrange two anchovies on each. Sprinkle each with ¼ teaspoon oregano, 1 tablespoon olives, 2 tablespoons Swiss cheese, and 1 tablespoon Parmesan. Broil about 4 inches from heat source, just until cheese begins to melt. Serve immediately.

*Bread Alternatives:* English muffin halves or French bread slices.

# TUNA CAPONATA

*A colorful, flavorful Italian-style tuna filling. For an even quicker version, use your favorite prepared oil and vinegar dressing.*

Makes 2 cups filling, or enough for 2–3 sandwiches

- 1 6½- or 7-ounce can chunk light tuna, drained and flaked
- 1 6-ounce jar marinated artichoke hearts, drained, quartered
- 2 tablespoons sliced pitted ripe olives
- 2 tablespoons sliced pimiento-stuffed green olives
- 2 tablespoons chopped red bell pepper or pimiento
- 2 tablespoons capers, drained
- 2 tablespoons wine vinegar
- 1 clove garlic, minced
- ½ teaspoon dried basil, crumbled
- ½ teaspoon dried oregano, crumbled
- 3 tablespoons olive or vegetable oil
- 2–3 hard rolls

Gently stir together tuna, artichokes, olives, bell pepper, and capers. Combine vinegar, garlic, basil, and oregano. Whisk in oil. Pour over tuna mixture and toss gently to coat thoroughly. Split rolls horizontally; hollow out bottom portion slightly. Fill with tuna mixture. Top with remaining half of roll.

*Variation:* Add 5 cherry tomatoes, cut in half, to the tuna mixture. Line roll with lettuce.

*Bread Alternatives:* French or Italian bread loaf (cut into 4- or 5-inch lengths, then split horizontally) or pita breads.

# TURKEY & CHEDDAR PITA

*A combination of favorite sandwich ingredients—tastes great on most any bread, too.*

Makes 2 cups filling, or enough for 2 sandwiches

- 1 cup sliced mushrooms
- 1-2 tablespoons butter or margarine
- 1 cup cubed cooked turkey
- 3 slices bacon, cooked crisp and crumbled
- 1 cup shredded cheddar cheese
- 1 medium tomato, chopped
- 2 pita breads, about 6 inches in diameter
- Sour cream or plain yogurt (optional)

Cook mushrooms in butter in medium skillet over medium heat just until tender, about 3 minutes; stir occasionally. Remove from heat. Stir in turkey, bacon, cheese, and tomato. Toast pitas. Cut each in half to form pockets, and fill with turkey mixture.

*Variation:* Do not toast pitas. Fill each half with turkey mixture and wrap in foil. Place upright in 350°F oven; heat for 15 minutes, or until heated through and cheese melts.

*Bread Alternatives:* whole wheat rolls (great for the heated variation), heated tortillas, toasted English muffins, or bagels (which make a super open-face sandwich).

# TURKEY WITH HONEY-MUSTARD

*Ordinary ingredients come together to make a gourmet sandwich bursting with a different, but delicious flavor profile.*

Makes 2 sandwiches

- **2 tablespoons Dijon-style mustard**
- **2 teaspoons honey**
- **4 slices raisin bread**
- **Chutney, finely chopped**
- **2 Swiss cheese slices**
- **Turkey, smoked turkey, or ham slices**
- **Butter or margarine, softened**

Combine mustard and honey; stir to mix well. Spread one side of each slice of bread with honey-mustard mixture. Spread 2 slices, mustard side up, with chutney (to taste), and top with slice of cheese and as much turkey as desired. Top with remaining bread, mustard side down. Spread outsides of bread lightly with butter. Place in large skillet over medium heat. Cook about 3 minutes or until toasted; turn and cook 3 minutes longer until bread is toasted and filling is warm. Reduce heat if necessary to prevent overbrowning.

*Variation:* Use two croissants, split horizontally. Layer bottom half with honey-mustard mixture, chutney, cheese, and turkey as above. Top with remaining half of croissant. Wrap in foil. Place in 350°F oven for about 15 minutes or until heated through.

*Bread Alternatives:* bagels or whole wheat rolls.

# CRANBERRY-TURKEY CROISSANT

*Heated croissants are a nice touch. Make extra Orange Cream Cheese to spread on bagels and English muffins for a quick and luscious breakfast treat.*

Makes ⅓ cup Orange Cream Cheese, or enough for 4 sandwiches

- 1 3-ounce package cream cheese, softened
- 1 tablespoon finely chopped walnuts or pecans
- 1 teaspoon grated orange rind
- 1-2 teaspoons honey (optional)
- 4 croissants
    Whole cranberry sauce, cranberry conserve, or cranberry jelly
    Turkey breast slices

To prepare Orange Cream Cheese: combine cream cheese, nuts, orange rind, and honey; stir to mix well. (Quantity can be doubled, and refrigerated for later use.)

Split croissants horizontally. Spread bottom half of each with Orange Cream Cheese. Spread cranberry sauce over cream cheese to taste. Top with turkey and remaining half of croissant.

*Bread Alternatives:* Vienna or other white bread (cut into 1-inch-thick slices), cranberry quick bread or muffins, or English muffins.

# PESTO CHICKEN

*The fresh flavor of pesto mayonnaise also makes a great bread spread for sliced chicken, turkey, or ham sandwiches. For a change of pace, make a sandwich of pesto mayonnaise and prosciutto.*

Makes 2¼ cups filling, or enough for 2–3 sandwiches

- 1–2 **garlic cloves**
- ⅔ **cup mayonnaise**
- ⅓ **cup packed fresh basil leaves**
- 2 **tablespoons chopped parsley**
- 2–4 **tablespoons grated Parmesan cheese**
- 1 **tablespoon lemon juice**
- **Dash salt**
- 2 **cups cubed cooked chicken**
- ⅓ **cup toasted pine nuts or walnuts**
- 2–3 **hard rolls**

Mince garlic in food processor with steel blade. Add mayonnaise, basil, parsley, cheese, lemon juice, and salt to work bowl. Process until smooth. Toss pesto mayonnaise with chicken to coat thoroughly; stir in pine nuts. Split rolls horizontally. Spread chicken filling on bottom half of each roll. Top with remaining half of roll.

*Bread Alternatives:* French or Vienna bread (cut into ¾-inch-thick slices), sourdough rolls, or pita breads.

# SUNFLOWER CHICKEN SALAD

*Sunflower seeds provide a great nutty flavor and crunch to chicken and vegetable salad.*

Makes about 2½ cups filling, or enough for 3–4 sandwiches

- 1½ cups cubed cooked chicken, chilled
- 1 small tomato, chopped
- ⅓ cup chopped seeded cucumber (optional)
- ¼ cup toasted unsalted sunflower seeds
- ⅓ cup mayonnaise
- 2-3 tablespoons plain yogurt
- Celery salt, to taste
- Garlic powder, to taste just before serving
- 1 small avocado, chopped just before serving (optional)
- 3-4 hard rolls
- Spinach leaves

Combine chicken, tomato, cucumber, and sunflower seeds. Combine mayonnaise, yogurt, celery salt, and garlic powder; stir to mix well. Toss gently with chicken mixture to coat thoroughly. Just before serving, stir in avocado. (Avocado darkens quickly once it is cut.) Split rolls horizontally; hollow out bottom portion slightly. Line bottom half of roll with spinach leaves. Fill with chicken mixture. Top with remaining half of roll.

*Bread Alternatives:* onion rolls, pita breads, whole wheat or multigrain bread (cut into ¾-inch-thick slices).

# TANGY DILL CHICKEN SALAD

*Tangy yogurt-dill dressing makes a refreshing salad. Try it with turkey, too—either leftover or purchased from the deli if you're in a hurry.*

Makes 2 cups salad, or enough for 2 sandwiches

- ⅓ cup plain yogurt
- ⅓ cup mayonnaise
- ½ cup finely chopped seeded cucumber
- ¼ cup minced red or green bell pepper (optional)
- 1 tablespoon minced parsley
- 1 tablespoon fresh dill, or 1½ teaspoons dried dill weed
- 1½ cups coarsely chopped cooked chicken
- 2 pita breads, about 6 inches in diameter
- Alfalfa sprouts or lettuce

Combine yogurt, mayonnaise, cucumber, bell pepper, parsley, and dill; stir to mix well. Toss gently with chicken to coat thoroughly. Cut each pita in half to form pockets. Line pockets with sprouts. Fill with chicken salad.

*Bread Alternatives:* seeded bagels or croissants.

**GAZPACHO IN A ROLL**
*Spinach, tomato, cucumber, pepper and onion*

# TARRAGON CHICKEN CROISSANT

*Chicken with a delicious difference. Also great warm—just poach chicken, tear into strips, and add dressing for another sensational taste. Serve on a bread that will absorb the great dressing for maximum flavor in each bite.*

Makes about 1½ cups filling, or enough for 2 sandwiches

- 1 garlic clove, minced
- 2 tablespoons tarragon vinegar
- 1 tablespoon lemon juice
- 2 teaspoons Dijon-style mustard
- ½ teaspoon dry mustard
- Salt (optional)
- Freshly ground white pepper
- ¼ cup vegetable oil
- 1 tablespoon minced parsley
- 1 tablespoon capers, drained (optional)
- ½–1 teaspoon dried tarragon leaves
- 1½ cups cooked chicken strips, chilled, if desired
- 2 croissants, warm, if desired

Combine garlic, vinegar, lemon juice, mustards, salt, and pepper. Slowly whisk in oil to blend (mixture should thicken as oil is added). Stir in parsley, capers, and tarragon. Add chicken and toss to coat completely. Split croissants horizontally. Divide chicken mixture between bottom halves of croissants. Top with remaining halves.

*Bread Alternatives:* French or Italian bread loaf (cut into 4-inch lengths, then split horizontally).

# CURRIED CHICKEN SALAD

*Curry with all the condiments makes an outstanding sandwich. You'll probably have to double the recipe next time!*

Makes 2 cups chicken salad, or enough for 2–3 sandwiches

- ½ cup mayonnaise
- 1 tablespoon lemon juice
- 2 teaspoons curry powder
- 1½ cups cubed cooked chicken (smoked turkey may be substituted)
- 1 cup sliced celery
- ¼ cup toasted almonds
- 1 small apple or pear, chopped (optional)
- ¼ cup toasted coconut (optional)
- **2–3 kaiser rolls**
- **Leaf lettuce**

Stir together mayonnaise, lemon juice, and curry powder. Add chicken, celery, almonds, apple, and coconut. Toss to coat thoroughly. Split rolls horizontally. Line bottom half of roll with lettuce. Spread with chicken salad, and top with remaining half of roll.

*Bread Alternatives:* hard rolls, sourdough rolls or bread, whole wheat rolls or bread, pita breads, bagels, English muffins.

## THE GREAT GARBANZO

*A hearty meal-in-a-pita. Toss in chopped tomato if you like!*

Makes about 2½ cups filling, or enough for 3 sandwiches

- 1 cup cooked chicken, cut into 1-inch × ¼-inch strips (turkey may be substituted)
- 3 slices bacon, cooked crisp and crumbled
- 1 15-ounce can garbanzo beans (chick peas), drained
- 2 green onions, finely chopped
- 2 tablespoons vinegar
- 1 tablespoon minced parsley
- 1 teaspoon Dijon-style mustard
- ½ teaspoon sugar
- 3 tablespoons vegetable oil
- Lettuce
- 3 pita breads, about 6 inches in diameter

Combine chicken, bacon, beans, and onions. Stir together vinegar, parsley, mustard, and sugar; stir until sugar dissolves. Whisk in oil. Add to chicken mixture and toss to coat thoroughly. Cut each pita in half to form pockets. Line pockets with lettuce and fill with chicken mixture.

# GINGER CHICKEN PITA

*Fresh ginger lends distinct Oriental flair to this salad filling. Make ahead so flavors can blend.*

Makes 3 cups salad, or enough for 3 sandwiches

- 1½ cups cubed cooked chicken (turkey may be substituted)
- 1 cup bean sprouts
- ½ cup thinly sliced celery
- 1 medium carrot, shredded
- 2 green onions, chopped
- ¼ cup red wine vinegar
- 1 tablespoon sugar
- 1 tablespoon soy sauce
- 1 teaspoon minced fresh ginger
- Dash garlic powder
- 3 tablespoons vegetable oil
- 3 pita breads, about 6 inches in diameter

Combine chicken, sprouts, celery, carrot, and onions. Stir together vinegar, sugar, soy sauce, ginger, and garlic powder. Whisk in oil. Add to chicken mixture; stir to coat well. For optimum flavor, refrigerate several hours to allow flavors to blend, stirring occasionally. Cut each pita in half to form pockets. Fill with chicken salad.

*Bread Alternatives:* hard rolls (split horizontally and hollowed out slightly before filling).

## SUMPTUOUS STIR-FRY
*Bell pepper, mushrooms, cheddar, and onion*

# CABBAGE PATCH CRUNCH
*Red and green cabbage, tomato, alfalfa sprouts, and Muenster cheese*

# ANTIPASTO PASSION
*Artichoke hearts, salami, mozzarella, and red and green peppers*

# CRANBERRY-TURKEY CROISSANT
*Turkey, cranberries, walnuts, and orange cream cheese*

# 4
# GARDEN FAVORITES

Fresh produce from the garden, the farmer's roadside stand, or the supermarket makes wonderful sandwiches. And the benefits are many—good nutrition, easy preparation, and the color and crunch which add eye and palate appeal. Once you've had a taste of these great sandwiches, you will be ready to create some delectable garden delights yourself.

**SUMPTUOUS STIR-FRY**
**GAZPACHO IN A ROLL**
**CABBAGE PATCH CRUNCH**
**COOL SUMMER CRUNCH**
**EGGPLANT PITA**
**SPINACH SALAD SANDWICH**
**SUN-DRIED TOMATO WITH BASIL**
**CHUNKY GUACAMOLE**
**SOUTHWEST AVOCADO SALAD**
**VEGETABLE JAZZ**

# SUMPTUOUS STIR-FRY

*Top this nutritious sandwich any way you like, or leave it plain—it's as good plain as "dressed."*

Makes 2 cups filling, or enough for 2 sandwiches

- **1 small onion, cut into thin wedges**
- **1 tablespoon vegetable oil**
- **1 cup assorted bell pepper strips, ¼ inch wide (from red, green, and yellow peppers)**
- **1 cup thinly sliced fresh mushrooms**
- **Dash red pepper flakes (optional)**
- **Dash celery salt (optional)**
- **½ cup cubed Monterey Jack, cheddar, or brick cheese (optional)**
- **2 pita breads, about 6 inches in diameter**
- **Plain yogurt, sour cream, or salsa (optional)**

Cook onion in oil in medium skillet over medium heat 2 minutes. Add pepper strips and mushrooms. Cook and stir until vegetables are crisp-tender, about 2 minutes. Remove from heat. Sprinkle with pepper flakes and salt; stir in cheese. Cut each pita in half to form pockets and fill with vegetable mixture. Top with yogurt, sour cream, or salsa.

*Bread Alternatives:* whole wheat rolls, onion rolls, tortillas, or corn bread squares (serve open-face).

# GAZPACHO IN A ROLL

*This sandwich says summertime in every bite!*

Makes about 2 cups filling, or enough for 2-3 sandwiches

- 1 medium tomato, chopped
- 1 small cucumber, thinly sliced (about 1 cup)
- 2 tablespoons minced green bell pepper
- 2 tablespoons chopped red onion
- Wine vinegar and oil salad dressing
- 2-3 round hard rolls
- Spinach leaves

Combine tomato, cucumber, pepper, and onion. Toss with enough dressing to moisten thoroughly. For optimum flavor, refrigerate at this point for an hour to allow flavors to blend. Cut a thin slice horizontally from the top of each roll. Remove some of bread from the center of bottom piece, leaving a thin shell to hold filling. Line with spinach leaves and fill with vegetable mixture. Replace roll tops.

*Variation:* Add thin strips of salami, pepperoni, or ham to salad mixture. If desired, before lining with spinach leaves, inside of roll may be spread with softened cream cheese or a quick garlic butter. (To make garlic butter, season softened butter or margarine with garlic powder to taste.)

*Bread Alternatives:* whole wheat rolls (hollow out bottom portion slightly) or pita breads.

# CABBAGE PATCH CRUNCH

*Colorful and crunchy, you'll love this special lunchtime sandwich.*

Makes about 1¼ cups cabbage mixture, or enough for 2–3 sandwiches

- 2 tablespoons mayonnaise
- 2 tablespoons plain yogurt or sour cream
- 1 tablespoon vinegar
- 1 teaspoon Dijon-style mustard
- Dash garlic powder
- Seasoning salt, to taste
- ¾ cup shredded red or green cabbage
- ¼ cup chopped radishes
- ¼ cup chopped celery
- 1 green onion, finely chopped
- 4–6 slices whole wheat bread, cut ¾ inch thick
- 2–6 slices Muenster cheese
- Alfalfa sprouts
- Tomato slices

Combine mayonnaise, yogurt, vinegar, mustard, garlic powder, and salt; stir to mix well. Add cabbage, radishes, celery, and onion. Toss to coat thoroughly. Layer 1 slice cheese, cabbage mixture, sprouts, and tomato on one bread slice.

Add second cheese slice if desired. Top with second slice of bread. Repeat for remaining sandwiches.

*Variation:* Add slices of ham and/or turkey.

*Bread Alternatives:* bagels, English muffins, rye bread or rolls, or pita breads.

# COOL SUMMER CRUNCH

*Seasoned cottage cheese and fresh vegetables make a great lunchtime treat.*

Makes about 1 cup cottage cheese spread, or enough for 2 hearty sandwiches

- 1 cup cream-style cottage cheese
- 1 green onion, minced
- 2 tablespoons finely chopped green bell pepper
   Celery salt, seasoned salt, or seasoning blend of your choice
   Spinach leaves
   Thin tomato slices
- 4 slices whole wheat bread, cut $\frac{1}{2}$ inch thick

Combine cottage cheese, onion, bell pepper, and desired seasoning; stir to mix well. Layer spinach, cottage cheese mixture, and tomato slices on two bread slices. Top each with second slice of bread.

*Bread Alternatives:* onion rolls or bread, multigrain bread, rye bread or rolls, or pumpernickel bread or rolls.

# EGGPLANT PITA

*Eggplant aficionados will love this. It's worth the bit of extra preparation time.*

Makes 2 cups filling, or enough for 2 sandwiches

- 1 medium eggplant
- Vegetable oil
- 1 medium onion, finely chopped
- 2 garlic cloves, minced
- 1 tablespoon lemon juice
- 1 medium tomato, peeled, seeded, and chopped
- Salt and pepper (optional)
- 2 pita breads, about 6 inches in diameter

Cut eggplant in half lengthwise. Lightly coat with oil. Place cut side down on baking sheet. Bake at 350°F until tender, about 20–30 minutes. While baking eggplant, cook onion and garlic in 2 tablespoons oil over medium heat until tender and slightly browned. Cool eggplant slightly. Peel eggplant and finely chop. Add to onion and garlic; stir in lemon juice. Stir in tomato, salt, and pepper. Toast pitas, if desired. Cut each in half to form pocket and fill with warm eggplant mixture.

*Bread Alternatives:* French bread (cut into ¾-inch-thick slices and spread with garlic butter. Toast; serve open-face.)

# SPINACH SALAD SANDWICH

*Why not? It's a great salad combo!*

Makes about 2½ cups salad, or enough for 2–3 sandwiches

- ½ pound spinach, torn into shreds
- ¼ cup very thinly sliced red onion rings
- 1½ tablespoons red wine vinegar
- 2 teaspoons honey
- Dash salt
- Freshly ground black pepper
- 3 tablespoons vegetable oil
- 2–3 hard rolls
- 2 hard-cooked eggs, sliced
- 3 slices bacon, cooked crisp and crumbled

Combine spinach and onion. Set aside. Stir together vinegar, honey, salt, and pepper; whisk in oil. Add to spinach and toss to coat thoroughly. Split rolls horizontally. Layer spinach salad, egg, and bacon on bottom half of each roll. Top with remaining half of roll.

*Variation:* Add ⅓ cup cubed Swiss cheese and/or ⅓ cup chopped unpared apple to spinach mixture. *Or* add slice of Swiss cheese to each sandwich.

*Bread Alternatives:* pita breads, whole wheat rolls, or French or Italian bread loaf (cut into 4-inch lengths, then split horizontally).

# SUN-DRIED TOMATO WITH BASIL

*Assertive flavors of goat cheese, basil, and sun-dried tomatoes come together in this unique filling. Select a mild or pungent cheese as your taste dictates.*

Makes 2/3 cup filling, or enough for 3-4 sandwiches

- 2 tablespoons red wine vinegar
- 1 garlic clove, minced, *or* dash garlic powder
- 1 green onion, minced (optional)
- Freshly ground black pepper
- 3-4 tablespoons olive oil
- 1-2 tablespoons shredded fresh basil
- 2-4 tablespoons chopped sun-dried tomatoes, drained and patted dry
- 1/4 pound goat cheese, coarsely crumbled
- French bread loaf

Combine vinegar, garlic, onion, and pepper. Slowly whisk in oil to blend (mixture will thicken as oil is added). Stir in basil and tomatoes; gently stir in cheese. Cut bread into 3-inch lengths and split each horizontally or if you prefer, bread may be cut into 1-inch-thick slices for more bread and less crust. Spoon tomato mixture onto bottom half of bread. Top with remaining half of bread. (This sandwich also can be served open-face.)

*Bread Alternatives:* Italian bread or hard rolls.

# CHUNKY GUACAMOLE

*Great as a garnish for tacos or as a sandwich filling.*

Makes approximately 1 cup guacamole

- 1 medium avocado, peeled and pitted
- 1 tablespoon lime or lemon juice
- Dash hot pepper sauce
- Dash garlic powder
- 1 medium tomato, chopped
- Chopped ripe olives (optional)
- Crisp-cooked bacon, crumbled (optional)

Mash about half of avocado; chop remaining half; combine. Add lime juice, hot pepper sauce, and garlic powder; stir to mix well. Stir in tomato. Add chopped ripe olives and crumbled bacon to taste.

*Note:* Double recipe if guacamole is used as a sandwich filling.

*Bread Alternatives:* pita breads or bagels.

# SOUTHWEST AVOCADO SALAD

*A refreshing sandwich for cilantro lovers. Toss in crumbled cooked bacon or add a thin slice of ham to each sandwich for a great flavor variation.*

Makes about 1¼ cups filling, or enough for 2 sandwiches

- 1 medium avocado, peeled and pitted
- 1-2 tablespoons lime juice
- 1 medium tomato, chopped
- ¼ cup chopped green onion
- 1-2 tablespoons chopped fresh cilantro
- 2-3 English muffins, split and toasted
- **Salsa**
- **Sour cream**

Coarsely chop avocado. Stir in lime juice. Add tomato, onion, and cilantro; stir to combine well. Spread equal amounts on bottom half of each muffin. Add salsa and sour cream as desired. Top with remaining muffin half, or serve open-face.

*Bread Alternatives:* tortillas, bagels, or pita breads.

# VEGETABLE JAZZ

*Crisp-tender vegetables topped with cheese star in this open-face sandwich.*

Makes 2–3 sandwiches

- ¼ cup finely chopped onion
- 1 medium carrot, shredded
- Vegetable oil
- 2 cups small broccoli florets
- ½ cup thinly sliced mushrooms
- 1 small tomato, finely chopped
- 2–3 slices whole wheat bread, cut ¾ inch thick, toasted
- Shredded cheddar, Monterey Jack, Swiss, or mozzarella cheese

Cook onion and carrot in 1 tablespoon oil in medium skillet over medium-low heat just until onion is tender; stir frequently. Increase heat to medium; add additional 1–2 tablespoons oil if needed. Add broccoli; cook and stir just until crisp-tender, or to taste. Add mushrooms; cook and stir 1 minute or until desired doneness. Remove from heat. Stir in tomato. Place equal amounts of vegetable mixture on each bread slice. Sprinkle with cheese, and serve immediately.

*Variation:* Stir in shredded fresh basil or cubes of tofu for a wonderful change of pace.

*Bread Alternatives:* cheese bread, rye bread, onion bread, pumpernickel bread, pita breads, or flour tortillas.

# 5
# MORE SENSATIONAL SANDWICHES

Some of our favorites don't need recipes—the ubiquitous peanut butter and jelly, the classic club sandwich, pastrami on rye, the Reuben—and you probably don't need anyone to tell you how to make them. But everyone can use a new idea now and then—an unusual twist to an old favorite, or an altogether new sandwich. Following are some suggestions for great sandwiches. No recipes required.

- *Ham in a Biscuit*—spread with butter or favorite mustard.
- *Liver Pâté on a Bagel or Croissant*—sprinkle with chopped cooked bacon, chopped onion, cilantro, chopped radish, or ripe olives.
- *Cold Roast Pork on White Bread with Sesame Seed Crust*—spread with mayonnaise and layer with lettuce or creamy coleslaw.
- *Scrambled Eggs and Cheese (Cheddar, Brie, Swiss) on Toasted English Muffin or Bagel*—top with bacon, Canadian bacon, thin ham slices, chopped cooked salmon, lox, chopped green onion, tomato slices, or sautéed mushrooms.
- *Tuna Salad on Favorite Bread*—add celery slices, chopped apple, cucumber, onion, pineapple, bell pepper, herbs, shredded cheese, sliced olives, or crumbled bacon to the salad.
- *Chicken Salad on Wheat*—add walnuts, almonds, chopped apple or pear, sliced water chestnuts, shredded jicama, bell pepper strips, Swiss cheese cubes, chopped hard-cooked egg, chopped radish, chopped

tomatoes, dash of soy sauce and grated fresh ginger, or crumbled cooked bacon to the salad.
- *Chunky Peanut Butter on Wheat*—add mayonnaise, apple butter, banana slices, a sprinkling of granola, thinly sliced apple, raisins, chopped prunes, or dates.
- *Corned Beef on Rye or Onion Roll*—spread with hearty mustard and add sauerkraut, coleslaw, caraway seeds, spinach leaves, Swiss cheese slices, Monterey Jack cheese slices, onion, or tomato.
- *Sliced Roast Lamb on Herb Bread*—spread with homemade mayonnaise flavored with country-style Dijon-style mustard.
- *Prosciutto on a Heated Croissant*—add provolone cheese and sautéed mushroom slices.
- *Chili (with or without Beans) on a Corn Bread Square*—top with shredded cheddar and sliced green onion; broil just to melt cheese and serve open-face.
- *Cream Cheese with Chives on Wheat*—sprinkle with sunflower seeds; add thinly sliced cucumber, tomato, and finely chopped onion.
- *Canadian Bacon on Wheat*—add spicy mustard and sliced Monterey Jack cheese; grill.
- *Rare Roast Beef on a Croissant*—top with Brie, heat just until cheese begins to melt.
- *Smoked Turkey on Toasted English Muffin*—top with sliced Canadian bacon, Muenster cheese, and Dijon-style mustard; add leaf lettuce.

- *Creamy Crab or Shrimp Salad on a French Roll*—add crumbled cooked bacon, strips of green onion, cherry tomatoes (cut in half), and chopped bell pepper.
- *Shredded Carrot, Pineapple, and Raisin Salad on a Bagel*—spread with softened cream cheese; serve open-face.
- *Whipped Cream Cheese on a Heated Croissant*—add orange marmalade or favorite preserves for a great breakfast sandwich.
- *Pimiento Cheese on White*—combine shredded cheddar cheese, chopped drained pimiento, and lots of freshly ground black pepper; moisten with mayonnaise to make pimiento cheese. Add cooked crumbled bacon; grill.
- *Ham on Raisin Bread*—spread with chutney and green onion cream cheese; grill if desired.
- *Sliced Mozzarella on French Bread*—add tomato slices and shredded fresh basil; drizzle lightly with olive oil.
- *Monterey Jack Cheese Slices on Wheat*—add sprouts and thinly sliced tomato and spread with dill-yogurt-mayonnaise mixture.
- *Rare Roast Beef on Toasted English Muffin*—top with sautéed mushrooms and sour cream, which have been stirred together and gently heated.
- *Cream Cheese on Rye*—sprinkle with crumbled blue cheese; add a tomato slice and crumbled cooked bacon; grill.
- *Oriental-Style Stir-Fry in a Pita*—add minced fresh ginger for a refreshing taste. You may need to cut down on sauce amount to prevent a soggy sandwich.

# INDEX TO RECIPES

Antipasto Passion, 44
Asparagus Gratinée, 21
Basic Mayonnaise, 10
Blue Cheese-Walnut Spread, 27
Cabbage Patch Crunch, 68
California Dreamin', 50
Camembert and Pear Croissant, 25
The Chalet, 33
Chevre and Eggs Florentine, 28
Chunky Guacamole, 73
Chutney Lamb, 47
Cool Summer Crunch, 69
Cranberry-Turkey Croissant, 56
Curried Chicken Salad, 62
Deli Delight, 43
Eggplant Pita, 70
French Toast à l'Orange, 22
Gazpacho in a Roll, 67
Ginger-Apple Topper, 20
Ginger Chicken Pita, 64
The Great Garbanzo, 63
The Great Salmon Caper, 49
Grilled Caraway & Ham, 34

Honey Cream Cheese Crunch, 23
Honey Ham Salad, 32
Mushroom & Leek Croissant, 19
Never-Better Corned Beef, 42
Open-Face Steak & Mushrooms, 36
Pesto Chicken, 57
Picadillo Pita, 38
Pita Provençal, 52
Polish Sausage 'n' Kraut, 45
Pumpernickel Grill, 31
Regal Roquefort, 39
Smoked Salmon and Watercress, 29
Southwest Avocado Salad, 74
Spinach Salad Sandwich, 71
Sugar & Spice, 26
Sumptuous Stir-Fry, 66
Sun-Dried Tomato with Basil, 72
Sunflower Chicken Salad, 58
Sunrise Salad, 24
Super Sausage Supreme, 46
Taco Pita, 40
Tangy Beef Strips, 37
Tangy Dill Chicken Salad, 59

Tarragon Chicken Croissant, 60
Tuna Caponata, 53
Turkey & Cheddar Pita, 54

Turkey with Honey-Mustard, 55
The Ultimate, 35
Vegetable Jazz, 75